Great Women of the Suffrage Movement

by Dana Meachen Rau

Content Adviser: Jennifer Spencer,
Education and Collections Manager,
Sewall-Belmont House and Museum, Washington, D.C.

Reading Adviser: Rosemary G. Palmer, Ph.D.,
Department of Literacy, College of Education,
Boise State University

Compass Point Books ✦ Minneapolis, Minnesota

Compass Point Books
1710 Roe Crest Drive
North Mankato, MN 56003

Copyright © 2006 by Compass Point Books, a Capstone imprint.
All rights reserved. No part of this book may be reproduced without written permission from the publisher. The publisher takes no responsibility for the use of any of the materials or methods described in this book, nor for the products thereof.
Printed in the United States of America in North Mankato, Minnesota.
062015
009049R

 This book was manufactured with paper containing at least 10 percent post-consumer waste.

On the cover: A suffrage parade on May 6, 1912, in New York City

Photographs ©: Library of Congress, cover, back cover, 9, 10, 18, 23, 28, 29, 36, 37, 41; Prints Old and Rare, back cover (far left); APA/Getty Images, 4; The Granger Collection, New York, 5, 7, 8, 16, 19, 24; Sophia Smith Collection, Smith College, Photograph by Rockwood, 1440 Broadway, New York, NY, 6; North Wind Picture Archives, 12; Department of Rare Books, Special Collections and Preservation, University of Rochester Library, 13; Kean Collection/Getty Images, 14; Bettmann/Corbis, 15, 21, 33; Battle Creek Historical Society, 20, 22; Time Life Pictures/Mansell/Getty Images, 25; Special Collections Research Center, University of Chicago Library, 27; Iowa State University, 30; The Carrie Chapman Catt Collection, Bryn Mawr College Library, 32; MPI/Getty Images, 34; Stock Montage, Inc., 38.

Managing Editor: Catherine Neitge
Designer/Page Production: Bradfordesign, Inc./The Design Lab
Photo Researcher: Marcie C. Spence
Cartographer: XNR Productions, Inc.
Educational Consultant: Diane Smolinski
Library Consultant: Kathleen Baxter

Creative Director: Keith Griffin
Editorial Director: Carol Jones

Library of Congress Cataloging-in-Publication Data
Rau, Dana Meachen, 1971–
  Great women of the suffrage movement / by Dana Meachen Rau.
    p. cm.—(We the people)
  Includes bibliographical references and index.
  ISBN-13: 978-0-7565-1270-5 (hardcover)
  ISBN-13: 978-0-7565-1726-7 (paperback)
  1. Women—Suffrage—United States—History—Juvenile literature. 2. Suffragists—United States--History--Juvenile literature. 3. Suffragists—United States—Biography—Juvenile literature. I. Title. II. We the people (Series) (Compass Point Books)
  JK1898.R38 2005
  324.6'23'092273--dc22   2005002471

Visit Compass Point Books on the Internet at *www.capstonepub.com*

TABLE OF CONTENTS

QUESTIONING WOMEN'S ROLES

The United States is a democracy in which the country's people elect its leaders. Voting is an important right of all citizens. Until 1920, however, not all Americans had the right to vote.

Since men were the decision makers of the family, they did the voting. It was against the law for women to participate in elections. Many men believed women were too frail and simple to make choices for themselves. In fact, most women were not allowed to go to school or work outside the home. They were just

A suffragist urges women to vote in 1920.

4

expected to be good wives, mothers, and homemakers.

In the 1800s, some women began to ask questions about why they did not have the right to vote. After all, they lived in the United States. They should be able to take part in making decisions about their country.

Suffragists petitioned Congress for the right to vote in 1873.

The Declaration of Independence, the document that the Founding Fathers of the United States had written to declare the country's independence from Great Britain, stated that "all men are created equal." Women wanted to speak out and be sure they were not forgotten. Suffrage, or the right to vote, would give women a voice.

Thousands of women fought for suffrage. They were led by many outstanding individuals. This book includes the stories of some of these suffragists who worked hard to give women the right to vote.

Elizabeth Cady Stanton: Mother of the Movement

"All men and women are created equal."

—from the Declaration of Rights and Sentiments

by Elizabeth Cady Stanton

Elizabeth Cady Stanton (1815–1902) was always sensitive to the unfair treatment of women. Elizabeth was the daughter of a lawyer. Growing up in Johnstown, New York, she felt sorry for the women who sought help from her father. She learned that once a woman married, she became the property of her husband and lost many of her rights.

Unlike other girls of her day, Elizabeth went to school with

Elizabeth Cady Stanton in 1835

6

the boys and proved she could be as smart and athletic as they were. While other young women worried about marriage and home management, she attended the Troy Female Seminary to further her education.

Elizabeth had a sparkling personality that endeared her to many, including Henry Brewster Stanton. They married in 1840 and together worked for equal rights for black people. That same year, they attended the World Anti-Slavery Convention in London, England. But Elizabeth and the other women who attended were forced to sit behind a curtain and were not allowed to participate.

Only men were allowed to speak at the anti-slavery convention in 1840.

7

Elizabeth was stunned with the unfair treatment of women at the convention. While there, she met a woman named Lucretia Mott, who had also been told she could not participate. After they returned to the United States, Stanton, Mott, and three other women organized a convention of their own. It announced to the world that women were equal to, and should have the same rights as, men.

This first women's rights convention—held in Seneca Falls, New York, in 1848—launched the women's movement in the United States. More than 100 people, both men and women, attended the convention, where Stanton read a

Elizabeth Cady Stanton spoke at the first women's rights convention in 1848.

document the organizers of the convention had written called the *Declaration of Rights and Sentiments.* It listed the rights they felt women should have, including the right to vote, which was a radical idea at the time.

Elizabeth Cady Stanton with her daughter

Elizabeth Cady Stanton felt very comfortable in front of an audience. Many women across the United States read and heard of women's suffrage through her speeches and newspaper articles. From 1869 to 1890, Stanton served as president of the National Woman Suffrage Association, an organization that she helped found. Later, NWSA joined another group to form the National American Woman Suffrage Association. She served as its president for two years.

An 1896 political cartoon shows Stanton (left),
George Washington, and Susan B. Anthony floating
in the clouds at a suffragist convention.

Because she came from a wealthy family, Stanton easily gained the respect of middle- and upper-class ladies like herself. She was married and the mother of seven children. She proved to other women that a wife and mother could still have strong opinions about her country's leaders.

Elizabeth Cady Stanton fought not only for a woman's right to vote, but for other rights for women. Up until her death at age 86, she was never afraid to express her views. When she died, women were still denied many rights, including suffrage, but she fought to the end for better laws that would make women equal to men. She was an inspiration to those women who continued the campaign for suffrage.

SUSAN B. ANTHONY: INDEPENDENT AND STEADFAST

"Failure is impossible."

—*Susan B. Anthony in a 1906 speech in Baltimore*

Susan B. Anthony (1820–1906) grew up in a household where education was encouraged and women were equal to men. Throughout her young life, she met many abolitionists and women leaders.

Her family was Quaker, a religion that opposed slavery and violence and that allowed women to be leaders. From early on, Anthony questioned laws that took rights away from others.

Always eager to learn, Anthony attended school and became a teacher. She became involved in the temperance movement, which worked to ban the use of alcohol. Members of the temperance movement believed alcohol made men treat women poorly. At the meetings, however, Anthony was not allowed to speak because she was a woman.

The Quaker religion allowed women to take leadership roles.

Anthony got involved in the suffrage movement, and in 1850, she met Elizabeth Cady Stanton. They became lifelong friends and the perfect team. Stanton did the research, created publicity pieces, and wrote the speeches. Anthony, meanwhile, traveled the country to set up conventions, made speeches to gather support for the suffrage movement, and raised the money needed to keep the cause going.

Anthony never married. She did not want to give up all her rights to a husband. She was an example to others that a woman could have a fulfilling life without answering to anyone but herself. For this she was often criticized. People were not used to a woman with such strong opinions.

In 1869, Anthony and Stanton became upset when the 15th Amendment to the U.S. Constitution gave black men the right to vote but not women. They also wanted to take on other women's issues, such as equal pay for equal work, equal rights in

Susan B. Anthony

marriage, and the right to a better education. They created the National Woman Suffrage Association in 1869 to address these issues. Not all suffragists agreed with Stanton and Anthony. They were considered too radical.

In 1872, Anthony took a stand for women's suffrage. She tried to vote. She felt that the 14th Amendment to the Constitution, which said that citizens could vote, might also include women. So she took the chance and proudly placed her vote in Rochester, New York. Two weeks later, she was arrested and fined.

14   *Elizabeth Cady Stanton (left) and Susan B. Anthony*

Later, when rival groups of suffragists finally came together as the National American Woman Suffrage Association, Susan B. Anthony served as its president from 1892 to 1900. Suffragists looked up to her. Younger suffragists affection-ately called her Aunt Susan. Her steadfast loyalty to the cause of suffrage was admired and modeled by many.

Susan B. Anthony was the subject of a cartoon after she was charged with unlawful voting.

LUCY STONE: SPEAKING STATE BY STATE

"I must speak for the women."

—*Lucy Stone in an 1847 speech*

Lucy Stone attended Oberlin College.

Unlike Susan B. Anthony, Lucy Stone (1818–1893) had a traditional upbringing. Her parents believed the man should rule the home. Lucy did not agree. She wanted to attend college like her brothers. When her father would not pay for her to go, she worked as a teacher to raise the money. Oberlin College in Ohio accepted women,

16

and she became the first woman from Massachusetts to get a college degree.

During college, Stone enjoyed giving speeches, but she had to practice quietly. Public speaking was not acceptable for women. After graduation, Stone became involved in anti-slavery groups. Through these concerned people, she was also exposed to women's rights issues. Soon, she was lecturing on women's suffrage. Traveling the country, she spread the word. It was clear to all who heard her speak how devoted she was to the cause.

Stone did not want a household like the one she grew up in, where the husband ruled over his wife and children. When she met Henry Brown Blackwell, she realized that not all marriages had to be like that of her parents. Blackwell shared many of her ideas for equal rights for women. In 1855, they married and together fought for women's suffrage.

In the late 1860s, two amendments were about to be added to the Constitution. The 14th and 15th amendments

Lucy Stone

Henry Blackwell

18

would make former slaves citizens and give them the right to vote. But they defined voters as men. Stone and her husband fought hard to include women in the amendments.

They lost, but they believed the amendments were a step in the right direction. If the country was willing to make former slaves voters, then women were sure to be next. Other women's rights leaders, such as Stanton and Anthony, did not agree. They felt betrayed. Now was the time to get the vote, they argued. But Congress had refused to include a mention of women in the amendments.

Members of the women's movement could not agree on a course of action. So they split into two separate organizations. While Stanton and Anthony started the National Woman Suffrage Association to pursue a variety of women's issues, Stone and others based in Boston founded the American Woman Suffrage Association, which focused only on suffrage.

Stone believed that working state by state was the best way to secure the vote. At the time, individual states could grant their women citizens the right to vote. Stone gave speeches and gained support through the newspaper she published, *The Woman's Journal.* It was called "the voice of the woman's movement." Lucy Stone continued to be active in the fight for equal rights almost until the day she died at age 75.

A statue of Lucy Stone is part of the Boston Women's Memorial.

19

SOJOURNER TRUTH: WOMAN OF GOD

"Ain't I a woman?"

—*Sojourner Truth in an 1851 speech in Ohio*

A young girl named Isabella was born to slave parents in rural New York in the late 1790s. Since good records were not always kept, she was not sure of the exact year of her birth. She had a hard life, beaten and abused by her slave-owning masters. She watched as members of her family and even her own children were sold. With the help of a Quaker family named Van Wagener,

Isabella Van Wagener was treated like property and sold at an auction with sheep.

20

she escaped from the injustice of slavery. She chose to work for them and took on their last name.

While many things precious to her were taken away, Isabella Van Wagener (1797?-1883) never lost her faith in God. She often heard voices and saw visions, both of which she believed came from above. In 1843, she believed

Isabella Van Wagener changed her name to Sojourner Truth when she was about 46.

God told her to spread her faith and the idea of loving one another to whoever would listen. She changed her name to Sojourner Truth—"Sojourner" because she was on a journey, and "Truth" for her belief in God. She walked through the streets of New England, speaking at corners and stopping in at churches and meetings. When she reached Northampton,

21

Massachusetts, she met abolitionists and became deeply involved in the movement against slavery.

Sojourner Truth was a powerful speaker. Tall for a woman at 6 feet (1.8 meters), she had a loud speaking voice and a beautiful singing voice. In 1850, she attended a conference in Worcester, Massachusetts, led by Lucy Stone. There, Truth met major leaders of the women's suffrage movement.

Sojourner Truth felt that women's rights were closely tied to those of blacks. She became an important part of many women's suffrage meetings and made a convincing case for full equality.

In 1851, she gave an especially rousing speech. At a women's rights convention in Ohio, clergymen were yelling insults at the women.

FREE LECTURE!

SOJOURNER TRUTH,

Who has been a slave in the State of New York, and who has been a Lecturer for the last twenty-three years, whose characteristics have been so vividly portrayed by Mrs. Harriet Beecher Stowe, as the African Sybil, will deliver a lecture upon the present issues of the day,

Truth spoke out for women and slaves.

They believed a woman's place was in the home, not at a meeting where they talked about rights. Sojourner Truth gave her "Ain't I a Woman?" speech. In it, she listed the things she could do equal to or better than men, even though she was a woman. At the end of the speech, even the clergymen were applauding.

Sojourner Truth met with President Abraham Lincoln in 1864.

Sojourner Truth traveled to states in the East and West. As a woman and a black person, she was criticized more harshly than others. But she never stopped speaking about the injustices she saw in the United States.

23

IDA B. WELLS-BARNETT: PROUD TO MARCH

"Set the wheels of justice in motion before it is too late."
—Ida B. Wells-Barnett in a letter to the
Chicago Tribune, *1919*

Ida B. Wells (1862–1931) was a born leader. Raised in Mississippi during and after the Civil War, she became a teacher in her early teens to support her brothers and sisters after her parents died from yellow fever, a serious infectious disease.

She witnessed the unfair treatment of her fellow African-Americans. This inspired her to become a journalist,

Ida B. Wells-Barnett

24

Wells-Barnett led a crusade against lynching, in which innocent blacks were hanged.

where she could make her readers aware of what was happening in the South and elsewhere. She was half-owner and editor of the black newspaper the Memphis *Free Speech and Headlight.* Her articles discussed ways to improve the conditions of African-Americans. Many of her articles brought attention to lynching. Black men were being killed without cause. They were found guilty of crimes they did not commit and then killed for them.

Ida B. Wells married Ferdinand Lee Barnett, a lawyer in Chicago who was also involved in journalism and the community. She started black women's clubs, which met to talk about issues and enact positive change in their neighborhoods. They discussed changes to laws that kept black people from enjoying the same activities as whites.

Suffrage soon became an important issue for Wells-Barnett as well. She founded the first African-American women's suffrage organization, called the Alpha Suffrage Club of Chicago.

The point of suffrage was to give everyone an equal voice. However, there was prejudice within the suffrage movement, even by some of its leaders. They wanted to gain support from women all over the United States. But many Southern women would not join the movement if black women belonged. Wells-Barnett was often asked not to participate in certain events to keep the Southern women happy.

On one such occasion in 1913, Wells-Barnett and 60 women from her Chicago club went to the National American Woman Suffrage Association parade in Washington, D.C., where women from all over the country would be marching. She and other black suffragists wanted to

Ida B. Wells-Barnett and her four children

march with the women from Illinois. But parade organizers told her she could not. If black women attended, Southern women would not participate. The NAWSA leaders finally agreed to let black women march, but they had to march at the end of the parade.

27

Women on horses led the 1913 suffrage parade in Washington, D.C.

Wells-Barnett felt this was unfair. Suffrage was an important cause to her, and she wanted to represent her state. While the other black women who came with her did march at the end, Wells-Barnett walked to the sidelines. When the women from Illinois came past, she joined them and marched proudly next to the white women, united for the cause.

CARRIE CHAPMAN CATT: A WINNING PLANNER

"To the wrongs that need resistance, To the right that needs assistance, To the future in the distance, Give yourselves."

—*Carrie Chapman Catt*

Growing up in Wisconsin and Iowa, Carrie Chapman Catt (1859–1947) was an active and eager farm girl. She did not listen when her father told her that only men should vote or that men knew more than women. She said she became a suffragist when she was only 13.

When her father would not send her to college, she paid her own way. After graduating from what

Carrie Chapman Catt

The historic Old Botany building at Iowa State University was renamed Carrie Chapman Catt Hall in 1995.

is now Iowa State University, Catt became a teacher and a principal. She was promoted to superintendent of schools in Mason City, Iowa, which was an unusual accomplishment for a woman of her day.

After her marriage in 1885 to newspaper editor and publisher Leo Chapman, she started a career in journalism. Catt found the written word was a good way to discuss

30

women's issues, so she started a column to address them. Unfortunately, her husband died of typhoid fever a year after their marriage.

Catt started down a new path. She became very involved in suffrage in Iowa. In 1890, she attended a convention of the National American Woman Suffrage Association, which had recently formed when two rival groups merged. While leaders of the suffrage movement had disagreements in the past, she came in when women were united. That same year, she married George William Catt, who greatly supported her cause.

Carrie Chapman Catt was a strong leader. Her organizational skills were her greatest strength. She raised money and started suffrage groups. She felt that details and planning were vital to success. In 1900, when Susan B. Anthony stepped down as president of NAWSA, she chose Catt to replace her. Catt left the presidency in 1904 to tend to her ill husband, who died the next year. She spent most of the next eight years representing the International Woman Suffrage

The NAWSA board included Catt (back left) and Anthony (front right).

Alliance around the world. She returned as president of
NAWSA in 1915.

In 1916, Catt unveiled her "winning plan" to focus on
getting the right to vote in each state, while at the same time,
pushing for a constitutional amendment. She worked hard
to increase the number of states that allowed women's
suffrage. That way, if a constitutional amendment was

passed, many states would already support it. Catt's nationwide campaign to get women involved in suffrage paid off. She enjoyed the moment in 1920 when the 19th Amendment to the Constitution was passed, and women in every state could participate in elections.

Suffragists Carrie Chapman Catt (left) and Mary Garrett Hay cast their votes in 1920.

33

ALICE PAUL: A TIRELESS FIGHTER

"Help us make this nation really free."
—*from a leaflet written by Alice Paul*

Alice Paul (1885–1977) was a well-educated woman. Born in New Jersey, she earned several degrees from colleges in the United States. She left for England in 1907 to study there. While in England, she became interested in the Woman's Social and Political Union, a group attempting to gain more rights for women. They used militant methods to gain attention for their cause, including going on hunger strikes. Three times, Paul was arrested and put in jail for speaking her mind.

Alice Paul

Upon returning home to the United States in 1910, Paul was disappointed by the lack of progress made by the state-by-state suffrage movement. She joined the National American Woman Suffrage Association and tried to convince the suffragists that militant tactics like those used in England needed to be tried in the United States as well. Many women of the NAWSA did not agree. They were used to the slower, steady course toward suffrage.

But Alice Paul needed more immediate action. So she and another suffragist named Lucy Burns started their own group. In 1913, they founded the Congressional Union for Woman's Suffrage, which they later renamed the National Woman's Party.

That same year, Paul organized a parade in Washington, D.C., the day before President Woodrow Wilson's inauguration. Wilson did not yet support women's suffrage. About 8,000 suffragists marched down Pennsylvania Avenue. There were not enough police to keep the angry crowds away from the marchers, and more

*A newspaper reported on "disgraceful scenes"
at the Washington, D.C., parade.*

than 200 women were injured. But the women kept formation as best they could and furthered their cause.

Paul continued to put pressure on President Wilson to pass a constitutional amendment granting women the right to vote. In 1917, she organized daily picketing of the White House, where the president lived and worked. Women marched by its iron gates six days a week, from dusk until dawn, for almost two years.

In April 1917, the United States entered World War I, and the suffragists' pickets were soon seen as unpatriotic. Upset onlookers could not understand why the women

Protesters form a picket line at the White House in 1917.

would focus their attention on anything other than the war
being fought in Europe. People threw things, hurled curses,
and verbally abused the picketers. Instead of arresting the
abusers, police repeatedly arrested the protesters for block-
ing traffic. Alice Paul and others were taken to jail. Paul
was sentenced to seven months. While there, she refused
to eat and was force-fed three times a day through a long
tube down her throat. She continued taking a stand,
despite the horrible conditions of jail.

37

Supporters cheer as Alice Paul hangs a banner to celebrate the passage of the 19th Amendment.

Finally, Paul and the others were released. Even though it had been an ugly experience, Paul's arrest had helped the cause. Suffragists received a lot of attention. Paul celebrated when the amendment finally passed in 1920 granting women suffrage. But even then, her cause did not end. She drafted an Equal Rights Amendment to make women equal in every way in the eyes of the law and submitted it to Congress in 1923. She fought tirelessly for change and devoted her life to ensuring equality for women throughout the United States and the world.

ACHIEVING THEIR GOAL

In 1878, the amendment for women's suffrage was first introduced to Congress by the early women's suffrage leaders. But every year it was defeated.

By 1917, many states allowed women to vote because of the hard work of Carrie Chapman Catt and others who had fought for suffrage state by state. That

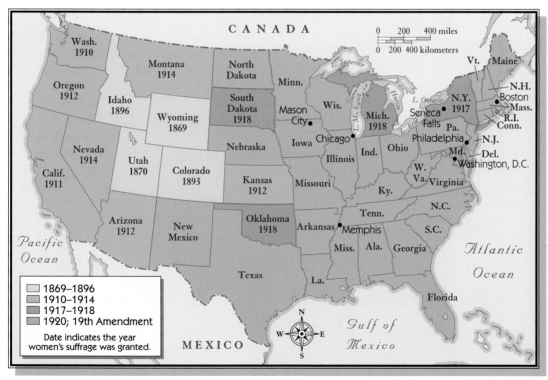

Some American women could vote before the passage of the 19th Amendment.

same year, newspapers were filled with the drama of Alice Paul and her fight to put pressure on the president.

Finally in 1919, Congress passed the 19th Amendment, and by the next year the necessary 36 states had approved it. On August 26, 1920, the amendment was added to the Constitution. Women could, at last, have a voice in their government.

In the election of November 1920, millions of women exercised their new right to vote. The desire to be considered equals—which began with Elizabeth Cady Stanton and other brave women at the 1848 convention in Seneca Falls—had finally been realized 72 years later. It was a long road to suffrage, and many suffragists along this road had battled hard. In the end, these great women of the women's suffrage movement preserved democracy in the United States and the equal rights of all of its citizens.

A 1920s poster urged women to use the vote granted by the 19th Amendment.

GLOSSARY

abolitionists—people who supported the banning of slavery

amendments—formal changes made to a law or legal document, such as the Constitution

Constitution—the document that describes the basic laws and principles by which the United States is governed

democracy—a form of government in which people elect their leaders

inauguration—a ceremony at which a president is sworn in to office

lynching—putting to death, often by hanging, by mob action and without legal authority

militant—aggressively active

picketing—standing or walking outside a place to protest or demand something

radical—favoring extreme changes or reforms

temperance—avoiding the drinking of alcohol

DID YOU KNOW?

- When Lucy Stone and Henry Blackwell married, Lucy kept her own last name and did not take on her husband's, as was the custom. Women after her who refused to take their husband's names were called Lucy Stoners.

- The changes for women included changes in fashion as well. In 1851, Elizabeth Cady Stanton's cousin, Libby Smith, started wearing pants under a short skirt that fell to her knees. It was more comfortable and less constricting than the long skirts most women wore. In 1852, Amelia Bloomer published a drawing of the new dress in a newspaper, and soon many women wanted to wear this outfit, which people called bloomers.

- The Equal Rights Amendment that Alice Paul first proposed in 1923 is still not part of the Constitution. It has been approved by 35 of the necessary 38 states. It reads:
  Section 1: Equality of rights under the law shall not be denied or abridged by the United States or by any state on account of sex.
  Section 2: The Congress shall have the power to enforce, by appropriate legislation, the provisions of this article.
  Section 3: This amendment shall take effect two years after the date of ratification.

IMPORTANT DATES

Timeline

1848	The first women's rights convention is held in July in Seneca Falls, New York.
1869	Elizabeth Cady Stanton and Susan B. Anthony form the National Woman Suffrage Association (NWSA); Lucy Stone and others form the American Woman Suffrage Association (AWSA).
1878	The Woman's Suffrage Amendment is introduced to Congress.
1890	The NWSA and AWSA unite to form the National American Woman Suffrage Association (NAWSA).
1917	Alice Paul and others are arrested outside the White House.
1920	The 19th Amendment is ratified.
1923	The Equal Rights Amendment is introduced in Congress.

44

IMPORTANT PEOPLE

ALICE STONE BLACKWELL (1857–1950)
Daughter of Lucy Stone and Henry Blackwell, she edited The Woman's Journal *for 35 years and was instrumental in uniting rival suffrage groups into the National American Woman Suffrage Association in 1890*

AMELIA BLOOMER (1818–1894)
Popularized changes in women's dress with "bloomers," which were loose pants worn under a shorter dress

LUCRETIA MOTT (1793–1880)
Quaker minister who fought against slavery and was an early reformer for women's rights

JEANNETTE RANKIN (1880–1973)
Montana resident who in 1916 became the first woman elected to the House of Representatives; she fought for many women's rights issues from within the government

VICTORIA WOODHULL (1838–1927)
Radical reformer who tried to run for president in 1872, calling for changes in labor, civil rights, and suffrage

WANT TO KNOW MORE?

At the Library

Bausum, Ann. *With Courage and Cloth: Winning the Fight for a Woman's Right to Vote.* Washington, D.C.: National Geographic, 2004.

Bjornlund, Lydia. *Women of the Suffrage Movement.* San Diego: Lucent Books, 2003.

Burgan, Michael. *Elizabeth Cady Stanton: Social Reformer.* Minneapolis: Compass Point Books, 2006.

Sullivan, George. *The Day the Women Got the Vote: A Photo History of the Women's Rights Movement.* New York: Scholastic Paperbacks, 1994.

On the Web

For more information on this topic, use FactHound.

1. Go to *www.facthound.com*

2. Type in this book ID: 0756512700

3. Click on the *Fetch It* button.

FactHound will find the best Web sites for you.

On the Road

Women's Rights National Historical Park Visitor Center
136 Fall St.
Seneca Falls, NY 13148
315/568-2991
To visit the site of the first women's rights convention and learn about the struggle for suffrage

The Sewall-Belmont House and Museum
144 Constitution Ave. N.E.
Washington, DC 20002
202/546-1210
To visit the headquarters of the National Woman's Party as well as the home to suffragist and equal rights advocate Alice Paul

Look for more We the People books about this era:

Angel Island
The Great Chicago Fire
The Harlem Renaissance
The Haymarket Square Tragedy
The Hindenburg

Industrial America
The Johnstown Flood
The Lowell Mill Girls
Roosevelt's Rough Riders

A complete list of We the People titles is available on our Web site:
www.compasspointbooks.com

INDEX

About the Author

Dana Meachen Rau is an author, editor, and illustrator. A graduate of Trinity College in Hartford, Connecticut, she has written more than 100 books for children, including nonfiction, biographies, early readers, and historical fiction. She lives in Burlington, Connecticut, with her husband and two children.